What Horses Teach Us...

LIFE'S LESSONS LEARNED FROM OUR EQUINE FRIENDS

GLENN DROMGOOLE

WILLOW CREEK PRESS

Minocqua, Wisconsin

© 2002 Glenn Dromgoole

Published by Willow Creek Press
P.O. Box 147
Minocqua, Wisconsin 54548

**Library of Congress
Cataloging-in-Publication Data**

Dromgoole, Glenn.
    What horses teach us / by Glenn
Dromgoole.
        p.   cm.
    ISBN 1-57223-579-9 (hardcover :
alk. paper)
    1. Horses-- Miscellanea.   2. Horses--
Pictorial works.   I. Title.
SF301 .D76 2002
636.1--dc21
                            2002009968

Printed in Canada

Dedication

For my wife, Carol, who loves horses and who had the idea for this book.

Acknowledgments

Special thanks to Sharon Matthews, Michie Cavuoti, Nancy Puckett, Maxine Grissom, Delbert Bailey, Janet Dromgoole, Russell Lackey, Ashlee Dietrich, and Amanda Reiter for their ideas and their time.

Table of Contents

On Getting Along with Others

If you're kind, it will show in your eyes.

Companionship may be found in unexpected places.

Appreciate diversity.

Give somebody a lift when you can.

Friendship transcends differences.

Building a
relationship
takes time and
effort.

I's nice to talk with someone who appreciates your point of view.

Good things come in small packages.

Savor a quiet moment with someone special.

$\int$tay close to your friends.

R espect your elders.

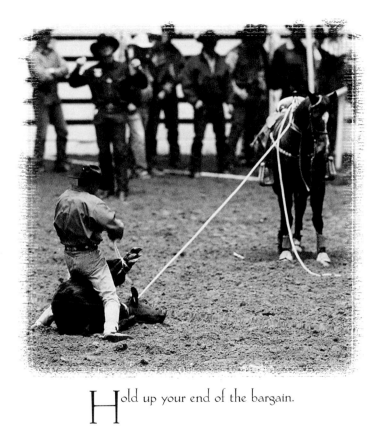

Hold up your end of the bargain.

A team has to pull together.

When you're the center of attention, try to stay humble.

Show your friends you appreciate them.

Be gentle
with children.

A kiss makes everything all right.

If you scratch my back, I'll scratch yours.

Spend more time with those you love.

Make new friends along the way.

On Personal Development

Sometimes we need a little nudge to get things done.

Don't let
obstacles
get in your way.

Blaze new trails.

Countless hours of practice go into minutes of perfect performance.

Take your responsibilities seriously.

U seful labor nourishes your soul.

Most of us are a bit awkward when we're young,
but we'll grow out of it.

$\mathcal{S}$tretch yourself.

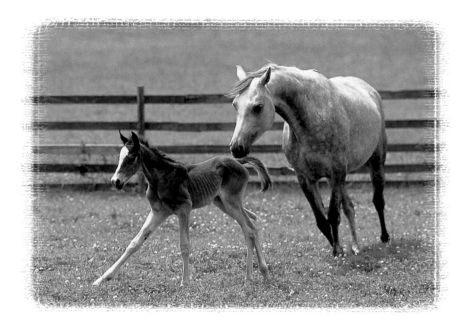

Teach your babies what they need to know.

The most valuable thing you'll ever earn is trust.

We have to learn to take turns.

There is a little show-off in all of us.

If you're going to succeed, you will need more than luck.

Carry your load without complaining.

Put your natural abilities to good use.

We all have it in ourselves to be champions.

$\int$tay in the saddle.

Savor the satisfaction of a day's work well done.

Always be open to learning new tricks.

Give it all you've got.

On Spiritual
Enrichment

Kick up your heels now and then.

Take pleasure in being outdoors.

Music soothes the spirit.

Cherish the simple things in life.

Life has its majestic moments.

Relish your independence.

Don't be afraid to lean on a friend.

Take time to smell the flowers . . .

And pick a few.

Renew yourself with the beauty of nature.

Find your mountain to climb.

A canter on the beach is good for the soul.

On Health

E at more apples . . .

. . . and carrots.

Drink plenty of water.

Include lots of fiber in
your diet.

Catch a few winks whenever you can.

Exercise often.

Always drink upstream from the herd.

Don't let a bad hair day get you down.

Early bonding sets the foundation of a healthy life.

Just say neigh.

Scratch what itches.

Nurture your relationships.

On Day-to-Day Living

Be alert to what's in the wind.

tay cool.

Everybody loves a parade . . .

Even the guys who have to clean up after it.

Keep your room clean.

The grass isn't always greener on the other side of the fence.

Try to mind your own business..

A smile is the easiest way to improve your appearance.

Take pride in your heritage.

$\int$ tand out from the crowd.

Keep your eyes on the task at hand.

Get as much horsepower as you can afford.

It's fun to pretend . . .

But there's nothing like the real thing.

Feel your oats now and then.

The race isn't over until you've crossed the finish line.

Whatever you do in life, try to enjoy the ride.